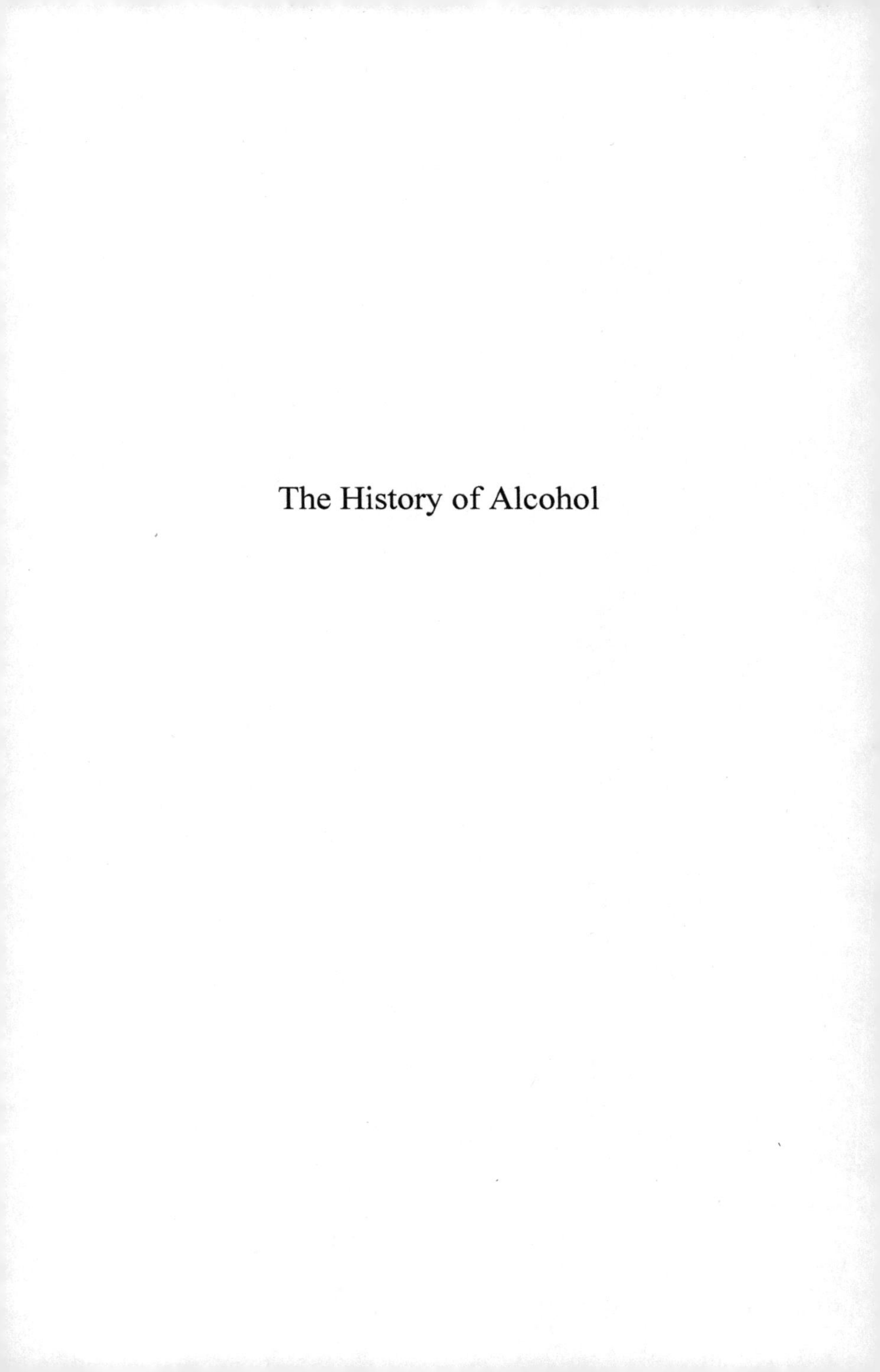

The History of Alcohol

Dr Charles Ernest Pellew

The History of Alcohol

(with illustrations)

LM Publishers

I.

In studying the history of alcoholic beverages we are at once brought face to face with the fact that there has hardly been a nation on the face of the globe which has not used some variety of stimulant or narcotic. In almost every instance this has been some form of alcohol, and in a few cases where alcohol has been unknown, and tobacco, opium, hemp, or some other drug used in its stead, the introduction of alcohol has been followed at once by its use and, alas! its abuse. A curious example of this is given in the account of Henry Hudson's famous voyage in 1609,. when he discovered the Hudson River. The Indian chief and warriors waited for him on the shore of Manhattan Island, prepared to sacrifice to the great "manito in red." He landed, with a few of his crew, and pouring out some rum into a glass, drank it to their health, and then passed a cupful round to the Indians. One after another they shrank from it, evidently fearing that it contained a deadly poison. At last one, bolder than the rest, drank it down, and soon began to reel and stagger, and finally fell. His companions were horror-struck. But soon he recovered himself, and described his drink in such glowing terms that they all begged and implored for their share, and, before Hudson left, they had all become intoxicated.

In other words, there seems to be a natural craving by man for some drug which shall "drive dull care away," and, as alcohol possesses this power, it has been used from the earliest ages and is still being used by rich and poor, high and low, civilized and savages, in more or less complete disregard of the evil effects of overindulgence.

The earliest historical records which have come down to us—the sacred classics of China, India, Judea, and Persia—all give details about the use and abuse of alcoholic beverages. The Chinese made use both of wine from grapes and of a beer made from rice, somewhat like the present *saki* of Japan; and, if we can believe their writings, intemperance was not at all confined to the lower classes, but in many instances proved the disgrace and the ruin of the reigning dynasties.

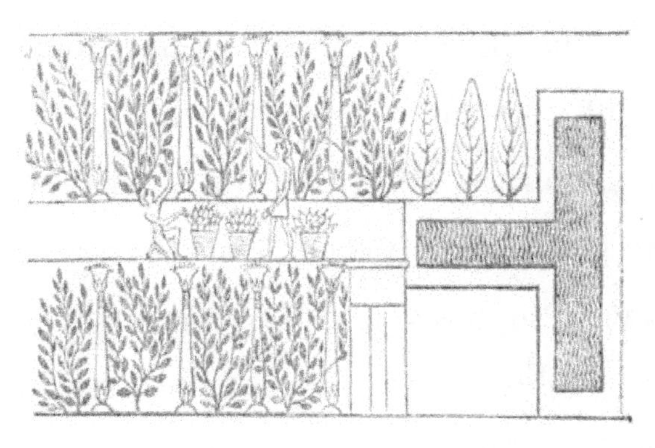

EGYPTIAN VINEYARD, WITH RESERVOIR OF WATER. (Wilkinson.)

The Rig-Veda, or sacred books of the ancient Brahmans, give us many details about the Hindu drinking customs, which were, among the upper classes at least, closely connected with their religious observances. The common people drank a variety of beer, known as *sura*, made from rice, barley, honey, and other ingredients. This was cheap and freely used for intoxicating purposes, and was, accordingly, in great disrepute among the priesthood and rulers, who made most stringent rules and regulations against it. But they were full of the praises of the sacred wine, *soma*, made from the juice of certain plants, which, after fermentation, was offered as a libation to their favorite gods, Indra, Vishnu, and others. These deities were supposed to drink *soma* freely, and to be highly gratified at the resulting intoxication. These exercises were particularly pleasant because it was not necessary, in order to honor the gods, to pour out all the wine upon the altar, but the act of devotion might be equally well performed by the worshipers drinking the libations themselves. Of course, the pleasant after effects were considered as solely due to the divine favor, and not to any ingredient common also to the vulgar *sura.*

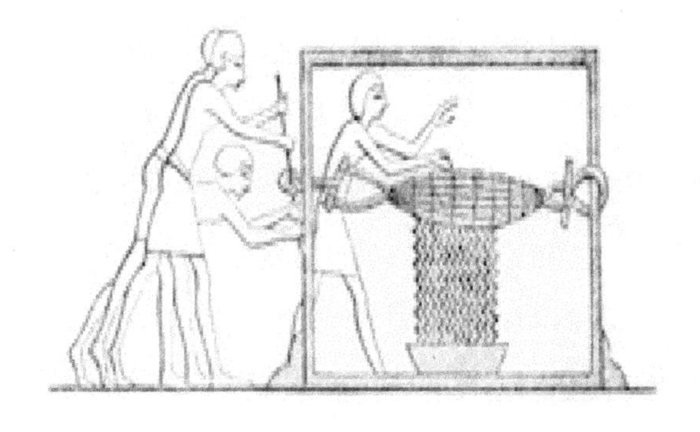

WINE PRESS OF MATTING. (Wilkinson.)

In the Bible we find frequent references to both the good and the evil effects of wine. In such marked contrast do some of these passages stand that serious effort has been made, by many well-intentioned moralists, to attribute all the favorable comments—"Wine that maketh glad the heart of man," "Thou hast put gladness into their hearts since the time that their corn and wine and oil increased," and the like—to unfermented grape juice or to the fruit itself, and to apply to the fermented juice, the wine of our everyday life, only the passages, so well known and so frequently quoted, of condemnation. Some grounds for their belief exist in the fact that two Hebrew words, *yayin* and *tirosh,* occurring in the Old Testament, are both translated in the authorized version as "wine," although *yayin* is almost always mentioned with scorn and contempt and *tirosh* with approval. But this is not always the case. The substances meant by both words are condemned alike in a chapter in Hosea (Hosea, iv, 2). And, furthermore, it is very doubtful whether the unfermented grape juice is not mentioned under an entirely different word, *debish,* translated as honey. In that hot climate, with no glass jars and rubber stoppers in which the sterilized grape juice could be preserved, and with no antiseptics to delay or prevent fermentation, the fresh grape juice must have been at once boiled down to a thick sirup, or it would have begun to ferment in half an hour. That is the present practice in Syria, and the resulting *debs* is used to this day as a substitute for honey or sugar for sweetening purposes. And our respect for the wisdom of King David and other great men of Judea hardly permits us to think that their enthusiastic language was used about a sweet, cloying sirup.

PRESSING THE GRAPES AND STORING THE WINE. (Wilkinson.)

There is no reason at all to doubt that the Greek word *οἶνος,* used in the New Testament, refers to the ordinary fermented wine; and, on the whole, it seems evident that in both Old and New Testament the commendations and denunciations refer to the use and abuse of alcohol, respectively, rather than to any specific differences between the beverages employed.

The ancient Egyptians at a very early date discovered the art of making barley wine, or, in other words, true beer, as well as grape wine.

They have left evidences of this, not only in their writings and in the tales of early travelers like Herodotus, but also in several remarkable series of mural paintings found on their monuments. The most interesting of these are at the tombs of Beni-Hassan, where, some five thousand years ago, the Egyptian artists amused themselves by portraying the scenes of everyday life in a most graphic manner. We find there pictures of vineyards, with the vines carefully trained on trellises, and watered from artificial reservoirs.

TAKING WINE LIKE A GENTLEMAN. (Wilkinson.)

We find several varieties of wine presses—some for treading the grapes, some for pressing the grapes by twisting them tight in a bag. We can see how they poured the fresh wine into jars for fermentation and storage. We can watch them drinking their wine like gentlefolk, in the bosom of their family, with wife by the side and children on the knee. And, finally, we find pictures of them using wine like beasts—men being carried home from supper on the backs of slaves; women staggering round, hopelessly and indecently intoxicated. Verily "there is nothing new under the sun."

AFTER A SUPPER. (Wilkinson.)

The ancient Persian writings, the Zend Avesta, dating back to the period of Zoroaster, possibly 4000 to 6000 B. C., contain like the Rig-Veda many references to a sacred drink, *homa,* and a popular drink, *hura.* Wine seems to have been of somewhat later discovery, but, once introduced, proved extremely popular. The lowlanders, living in the rich, warm plains of Asia Minor, were especially addicted to its use, and the temperate young prince Cyrus, coming down from the mountains with his Persian warriors, found little difficulty in routing the effeminate Medes. But the attractions of luxury proved too strong for them, and, in a few generations, both rulers and people had badly degenerated. The famous Xerxes, the Great King, the descendant of Cyrus and monarch of Asia Minor, left as his epitaph no great record of valiant deeds, but the sole fact that "he was able to drink more wine than any man in his dominions." Small wonder, then, that his forces were so easily routed by the Greeks.

For, of all races that have yet appeared, the Greeks have been best able to use alcoholic beverages freely and yet with temperance.

A WOMAN INTOXICATED. (Wilkinson.)

Their land was fertile and their crops varied, and they early learned how to prepare intoxicating drinks from barley, figs, the palm, and other sources. And their wines, especially those from the Greek islands, have retained their reputation, not for hundreds but for thousands of years. The vine was widely cultivated, and valued as one of the greatest gifts of the gods to man; and yet, such was their respect for the human body and such their dread of injuring it by excesses, that we find that, in their golden age at least, alcohol was used and not abused.

Their strongest drink, we must remember, was natural, unfortified wine, containing no more alcohol than our present clarets and hocks. And yet they never drank it pure; they always added water to it, or rather, added it to water. Some of their wines, the Pramnian and Maronian, for instance, were of such strong flavor as to be mixed in the proportion of one to fifteen or one to twenty parts of water. The average dilution was one to five, or one to four. When the young bloods of Athens had a supper party they would elect a "master of the feast," who sat, crowned with flowers, at the head of the table, and set the pace for the festivities. A very festive youth would sometimes at these occasions order the wine one to three, or even two to three. To drink wine unmixed—well, that was *ἐπισκύθισαι,* to act like a Scythian, to be a beast and a barbarian.

SLEEPING DIONYSOS. (From Greek bas-relief in the Campana Collection.)

It is not to be supposed from this that drunkenness was unknown, but in the golden age of Greece it was both uncommon and despised. Drinking with them was different from drinking among other nations; they drank for exhilaration, not for intoxication. This can be recognized at once from the character and position of Dionysos, their god of drink, corresponding to the Roman Bacchus. No drunken debauchee was he. His statues represent him as a laughing, innocent child, as a beautiful, graceful youth, as a finely developed adult, and even as a gentle, refined, full-bearded man, the patron of literature and the drama. For Dionysos was one of the greatest gods of Greece. At the vintage in the autumn all was fun and jollity, and in his honor rude, humorous plays were acted by the country people. Hence developed the "comedy," so named from *κῷμος,* the country cart from which the actors at first held forth. In the spring, at the opening of the new wine, occurred the great Dionysiac festival. Every one flocked to Athens, from the countryside, from all Greece, from the whole civilized world; and there, in the great Theater of Dionysos, the marble seats of which are still standing under the walls of the Acropolis, were acted the glorious tragedies of Æschylus, Sophocles, and Euripides, the noblest masterpieces of ancient literature.

But after Athens and Sparta, and later Thebes, had wasted their resources and exhausted their energies against each other, a new and fierce and semibarbarous race came down from the mountains and conquered the whole of Greece. Under the famous King Philip of Macedon the weak and scattered clans united, learned the art of war, and rapidly overthrew the more civilized and cultivated lowlanders. This marked the end of Grecian temperance. The Macedonian nobles were always heavy drinkers, and toward the end of his career they were encouraged in their habits by the king himself.

DIONYSOS, FROM THE CHORAGIC MONUMENT OF LYSICRATES.
(From The Antiquities of Athens, Stuart and Revett. 1762.)

Many stories have been handed down to us about the royal drinking bouts. One, which has passed almost into a byword, relates to a famous philosopher, who brought a lawsuit, in which he was a party, up before the highest court, the king himself. The case was heard and the judgment given against him. "I appeal," shouted the old man. "Whom do you appeal to?" said Philip, "I am the king!" "I appeal," said the other, "from Philip drunk to Philip sober." And the next day the case was heard over again, and decided in the appellant's favor.

Another episode, which bade fair to have very serious results, happened the year before he died. He had recently divorced his wife Olympias, the mother of Alexander the Great, and was celebrating his marriage to a new wife, Cleopatra.

SATYR PUNISHING A SAILOR, FROM THE CHORAGIC MONUMENT.

At the wedding banquet, where the wine flowed very freely, her uncle Attains made some insulting remarks about the young prince Alexander, who at once rose in his place at the table and threw a goblet at his head. This enraged the king, who sprang from his seat, drew his sword, and rushed at his son to kill him. But, in his rage and intoxication, Philip slipped and fell to the ground. Then Alexander, rather unfilially, shouted out: "See now, men of Macedon, this man, who is preparing to cross from Europe to Asia, cannot step from one couch to another without falling!"

When Alexander came to the throne, a year later, the improvement in manners was but temporary. At first, indeed, the young king, with his companions in arms, devoted all their energies to affairs of state and war. Two years after he came to the throne he crossed the Hellespont, and with a small but picked army routed the vast, unwieldy hosts of the Great King. In a few campaigns he conquered Asia Minor, and even led his victorious forces into India. But with success came intemperance, and his brief and glorious career closed in disgrace.

In the garb of Dionysos, accompanied by a band of drunken roisterers, he entered Carmania in triumph. At Samarcand, inflamed by wine, he killed with his own hand his friend Clitus, who had saved his life at the battle of the Granicus. At Persepolis, in a drunken frenzy, urged by dissolute companions, he set fire to the famous palace of the Great Kings, and although, sobered by the result, he urged his soldiers to the rescue, it burned to the ground.

His most famous exploit in this line took place, during the last year of his life, at the tomb of Cyrus, near Pasargadæ in Persia. He attended here the immolation of a famous Hindu philosopher, Calanus, who had followed him from India, and now, falling sick, burned himself alive on a great funeral pile. On his return from the ceremony Alexander asked many of his friends and chief officers to supper, and that night organized a great drinking contest, offering a gold crown to the victor. A young nobleman called Promachus took the first prize, with the respectable measure of some fourteen quarts of wine, and others followed close behind him. But a cold wind came up that night, chilling the revelers to the bone, and Promachus and some forty of his competitors died from the effects of cold and drunkenness combined.

MÆNADS IN A DYONISIAC FRENZY. A great figure of this sort, with splashes of blood on the garments, was one of the chief ornaments in the Dionysiac Theater. (From the Campana Collection.)

This course of life could not last long. His soldiers murmured, his officers grew unruly, his own strength failed; and, in his thirty-second year, after a drinking bout that lasted for two days and nights, a sudden attack of fever ended his career. Turning from Greece to Rome, we find the same general course of events. At first the Romans were a band of fierce banditti, fighting first for life, then for conquest, against the surrounding tribes. During the few hundred years that this struggle continued the Romans were a temperate, a painfully temperate race. We read that wine was scarce and poor, and, such as it was, reserved exclusively for the men, and for men over thirty. Women were forbidden to use it under pain of death, for the alleged reason that it was an incentive to licentiousness. According to Pliny, this last law was by no means a dead letter. Women were obliged to greet all their male relatives with a kiss on the mouth, so that it could be told if they had been at the wine cellar. He quotes the case of one Ignatius Mecenius, who cudgeled his wife to death for this offense, about B. C. 700, and was pardoned by Romulus for the deed; and he tells of another case, four hundred years later, where a Roman dame was starved to death by her relatives for similar reasons.

DELIVERING WINE. (From a wall painting at Pompeii.)

Later on, when they had conquered most of Italy, wine became more common, and when the Roman arms reached Greece and Asia Minor the country was flooded with it. We learn from contemporary writers that manners and customs changed within one generation. Old Cato used to tell how, at his father's table, only common Italian wine was served, and. that sparingly, while the Greek wine was handed round as a great luxury in small glasses at dessert. And before his death one general, Lucullus, returning from the East, distributed one hundred thousand gallons of fine Chian wine to the populace.

The later Romans cared more for their wine than for any other natural or artificial product of land or sea. Pliny mentions that there were one hundred and ninety-five varieties in general use, of which about eighty were of fine quality. Common wine was extraordinarily cheap and abundant, so much so that it was a jest of the poets that it was less expensive than water. Fine sweet dessert wines were imported in large quantities from the Grecian isles, Chios, Samos, Lesbos, Mitylene, and the rest. And the famous Italian vintages, the strong, fiery Falernian, the rich Massic, the sweet Alban, the Cæcuban, Setine, Pucine, and others, sung by Horace and Virgil and Lucretius, held the palm over all their rivals, and in many respects must have compared favorably with those of the present day.

But most of them would have been spoiled for our tastes by the curious substances which were added to them, for flavoring or as preservatives. For instance, both in Greece and Rome it was a quite common practice to mix honey, and also various spices, myrrh and aloes and cloves. A more surprising admixture was that of salt water, which, in small quantities, one to fifty or so, was believed to greatly improve the flavor of fine wines. Indeed, most careful directions are given by the old writers about the quality of this salt water. It must be drawn from the ocean, some three miles from shore, on a calm day, when the sea was at rest. Another, and to us barbarous, habit was that of adding resin or pitch or turpentine, either directly to the wine, or by smearing the wine vessels before filling them. This is done in Greece up to the present day, and the modern traveler is asked in the taverns whether he wishes "foreign wine" or "resined wine"—οίνος έξότικος or όίνος ρεαινήτής.

In one respect they were fully our equals. They appreciated the value of age. We still, some of us, have our wine cellars, and "lay down" our wines for aging. We smack our lips over a glass of Chăteau La Rose of '70, and think it old; while "Stuyvesant" or "Monticello" Madeira, from the beginning of the century, is doled out, on rare festal occasions, a few drops at a time, like a precious elixir.

But in Cæsar's day we hear of Hortensius, a well-known orator, leaving his heir ten thousand casks of good Greek wine in the cellar of his country house. Plump little Horace, always referring to his poverty, can still write to a friend and ask him to visit him at his humble cottage, and take a glass of Falernian laid down "Consule Planco," some thirty years ago. His patron Mæcenas used to give him wine—*Marsi memorem duelli*—that remembered the Marsian war, seventy or eighty years before. And we learn from Pliny that, in his day, there was still in existence some of a famous "cru" of wine, made in the consulship of Opimius, some two hundred years before. This wine, we read, was only used for flavoring other varieties. It was thick, so that it had to be dug out with a spoon, and dissolved in water, and strained before using it, and when the cover was taken off the jar it emitted a delightful, powerful fragrance which filled the whole room.

From the fall of the republic on, intemperance and licentiousness increased in Rome with rapid strides. Nothing more was heard of the old laws; the women drank just as heavily as the men. All the writers—Pliny,

Juvenal, Seneca, Tacitus, Athenæus, and many more—are full of bitter complaints against the prevailing habits. No order, no decency, was observed at their feasts. They rapidly became regular drinking bouts, where not only host and guests, but even the freedmen and slaves, drank themselves to unconsciousness.

Prizes were commonly offered, at these, to the heaviest drinkers, and it was customary to use drugs to increase the normal capacity for liquor. A separate chamber adjoining the dining room bore the suggestive name of *vomitorium.* The emperors themselves did not disdain to encourage these orgies. Under Claudius a certain Caius Piso was promoted at court for drinking consecutively for two days and nights. One man, Torquatus, was actually knighted under the name of Tricongius, or "Three-gallon Man," for taking that quantum of wine, so it was said, at a single draught. The populace, the home army, and the court were all equally intemperate; and it is no wonder that, when once the outer defenses of the empire were broken through, the rest collapsed and fell to pieces before the onslaughts of the hardier, even if no less intemperate, Northern races.

II.

It is a curious fact that, although intoxicating beverages have been known and used from time immemorial, alcohol itself was not discovered until after the fall of the Roman Empire, and, when once discovered, it was not used for intoxicating purposes for many hundred years. Pliny, in his Natural History, written about A. D. 50, mentions that oil of turpentine could be extracted from the crude pitch by boiling the latter in open vessels and catching the vapors on fleeces, from which the condensed oil could be pressed. This marks the first beginnings of the art of distillation, which progressed but slowly, for, two hundred years later, we read that sailors were accustomed to get potable water from sea water by similar crude methods.

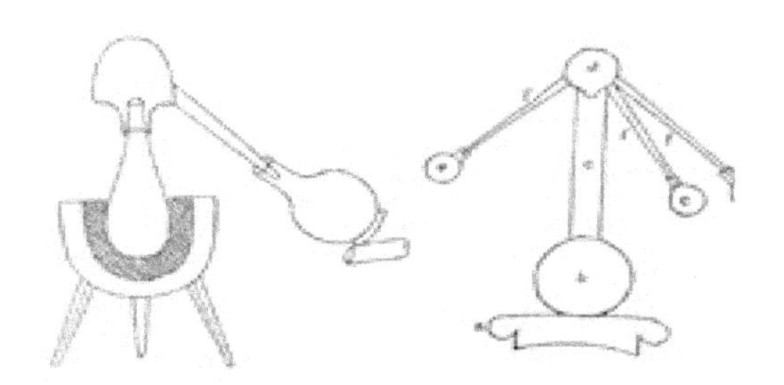

OLD STILLS USED BY ALEXANDRIANS

About this time there existed a flourishing school of alchemists at Alexandria, and it is probable that some of them had, or soon would have, developed the art further. But A. D. 287 the Emperor Diocletian destroyed their books and prohibited their studies, for fear lest by discovering the philosopher's stone, and hence learning to change base metals into gold, they might overturn the Roman rule. A more serious disaster befell the later Alexandrian School of Philosophy in the destruction of the famous Alexandrian Library by the Mohammedan general Amru, A. D. 984, at the orders of the Caliph Abu Bekr. "If the books agree with the Koran, they are not needed; if opposed, they are injurious." This was the argument which helped to put back civilization some centuries, and gave Literature, as well as science and medicine, a blow from which she has not yet recovered. It is curious to speculate what would be our present condition if only two or three of our recent advances—the discovery of galvanic electricity, for instance, or the germ theory of disease—had been made but one hundred years earlier.

As it was, the study of science had to be begun over again almost from the very foundation by the Arabians under a more enlightened rule. The famous Geber about the close of the eighth century mentions the term distillation, but it is doubtful whether he understood much more by it than the separation by beat of two metals of different melting points. Albucasis, a famous alchemist of the eleventh century, speaks of the process in less doubtful terms, and late in the thirteenth century the art of distillation and the preparation, properties, and uses of alcohol were clearly described by two European alchemists, Raymond Lully and Armand de Villeneuve.

OLD STILLS, FROM EARLY EDITION OF GEBER.

In view of the fierce and indeed not undeserved abuse that has been levied against distilled liquors, it is interesting to note that for some hundreds of years after its discovery alcohol was distinctly the most valuable product of chemistry. The old alchemists went wild over it. They wondered at its power of dissolving oils and resins and balsams, calling it *oleum vini* and *balsamus universalis,* and making with it varnishes and perfumes and cosmetics, by the sale of which they replenished their not overfilled purses. They admired the clear, colorless, smokeless flame with which it burned, and named it *sulphur cœleste,* in contradistinction to the ordinary or earthly sulphur, which burns by no means so pleasantly. They used it as a preservative, they used it for the preparation of their chemicals, and above all they used it as a medicine.

STILL FOR AQUA VITÆ, COUNTRIE FARME.

For during many hundred years this *aqua vitæ,* water of life as it was almost universally called, was the most valuable medicine in their large but inefficient pharmacopœia. Each alchemist, each physician, prepared his own elixirs, his own cordials, and claimed miraculous results for his own particular nostrums: but the basis of them all was the same—namely, alcohol, sweetened with sugar, and flavored by distillation or infusion with herbs and spices. Some of these "cordials" or heart remedies exist at the present day in the form of the various liqueurs. The Chartreuse and Benedictine are simply the same old medicines, prepared after practically the same old formulæ, that the Carthusian and Benedictine monks used to distill hundreds of years ago to give to the sick and feeble at their convent doors, or sell to the wealthy invalid who sought their treatment.

But the curious part of it is not that it should have been used as a medicine, but that it should have been used as a medicine exclusively. There seems to have been little or no idea of its intoxicating power. In Shakespeare, for instance, there is abundant mention of drinking and drunkenness.

HOUSEHOLD STILL, COUNTRIE FARME.

But Cassio, and fat Sir John, and the rest got tipsy on sack, and canary, and sherry, or, if of lower rank, on ale and beer, but never on spirits. Indeed, the only mention of distilled liquors in all his plays is in Romeo and Juliet, where the old nurse sighs, "Oh, for some strong waters from Venice!" to restore her energies. As an example of how long this state of affairs continued I may mention a well-known book. The Countrie Farme, published in England in 1616. This large and important work discusses in great detail all the varied occupations of a large country place. It describes carefully the wine industry, the culture of the vines and grapes, the preparation and the varieties of wine, and, while highly praising good pure wine as a beverage, the author is extremely careful to describe fully and with much emphasis the many evil effects which come from intoxication, and from constant as well as from overmuch winebibbing.

A. few chapters further on the author describes the art of distillation. He explains that a still room was a necessary adjunct to a well-equipped country house, and shows curious illustrations of stills, some of them with sixty or eighty retorts on one oven. He mentions the great variety of vegetable and animal substances from which extracts could be and should be distilled, but spends most of his time upon the distillate from wine. "For," says he, "the virtues of *aqua vitæ* are infinite. It keepeth off fits of apoplexie—it driveth away venime. . . . In wet and malarial climates everyone should take a teaspoonful, with sugar, before breakfast, to keepe off the ague," and so on. Not one word about intoxication—purely as a medicine.

TARTARS DISTILLING KUMYSS

It is not to be supposed from this, however, that the English did not have plenty of ways of getting tipsy. They had long been known as ranking next to the Germans and the Dutch for their drinking powers. The Saxons and the

Danes had both introduced into England the intemperate habits of the Northmen, and beer and cider, and mead or metheglin made from honey, were quite as efficacious in their way as stronger beverages. The Normans were a more refined and far more temperate race, and it is for this reason, in large part, that they conquered England so readily. The night before the battle of Hastings, so the old chroniclers tell us, was spent by the Saxons in drinking heavily and uproariously around their camp fires. "Next morning, still drunk, they recklessly advance against the enemy," so we read in the old monkish Latin, while the Normans, passing a quiet, peaceful night, were cool and well prepared for the decisive struggle.

ANCIENT STILL FOR EXTRACTION OF ESSENTIAL OILS AND PERFUMES.

Their habits, however, soon deteriorated, and they drank almost as heavily as their predecessors. In the reign of Henry I the nation suffered a grievous loss, from overindulgence in liquor, in the sad drowning of his eldest son, just married to a princess of France. The wedding party were returning to England on a galley, amid the rejoicing of both nations, and wine flowed freely on board, until even the seamen became intoxicated. As they were nearing the shore, the galley ran upon a sunken rock, and out of the whole company but one person escaped. The young prince, it was said, with his bride and some attendants had pushed off from the ship in a boat, but he insisted on returning to try to save his sister, when the boat was upset, and all perished together.

All during the middle ages, in the chronicles of Froissart, Holinshed, and others, we find records of the fact that our English ancestors, then as now, "liked a glass of good beer," and of wine too. Sir John Fortescue naively says, "They drink no water, except when they abstain from drinks, by way of penance and from principles of devotion."

GEORGE IV AS PRINCE REGENT. (Gillray.)

In 1498 the Spanish ambassador at the English court wrote to Ferdinand and Isabella to ask that Princess Catharine of Aragon, betrothed to Prince Henry, afterward Henry VIII, should learn to drink wine. This was a good-natured tip from the English king and queen, who wished their future daughter-in-law to know that "water in England is not drinkable, and, even if it were, the climate would not allow the drinking of it." Heavy drinking was not by any means confined to the laity, for there are constant complaints of the habits of the clergy, and especially of the religious orders. The drunkenness of both monks and nuns was one of the main excuses for closing the monasteries by King Henry VIII. Good Queen Bess did not frown on the practice either, for, in the records of her visit to Kenilworth, 1575, we read that the Earl of Leicester broached three hundred and sixty-five hogsheads of beer, besides any amount of wine.

Toward the end of her reign drinking increased, thanks to the habits acquired by the volunteers in the Low Countries; and under her successor, the stupid and pedantic Scotchman, James I, the court itself set an ugly example to the people of England. We read that, at a great feast given by the minister Cecil to the king and to a visiting monarch. Christian IV of Denmark, James was carried to the bed intoxicated, and

King Christian, less fortunate, rolled around very much under the influence of liquor and grossly insulted some of the ladies present. The latter, in their turn, before the evening was through, became quite as tipsy as the men, and, according to the testimony of an eye-witness, behaved most disgracefully. The nation sobered somewhat during the next reign and under the Commonwealth, only to return again to loose habits after the Restoration. And with the accession of the Dutch King, William, in 1688, the drinking assumed a more dangerous stage than ever.

For by this time people had at last learned that alcohol was intoxicating, and had also learned how to make it cheaply out of grain. Up to the seventeenth century all the *aqua vitæ*, was made from wine, and was therefore expensive. But now they were able to make it from beer; and not only in France, at Nantes and elsewhere, but in Switzerland, and especially in Holland, at Schiedam and other places, great distilleries were pouring out vast quantities of cheap and fiery spirits. Early in William and Mary's reign encouragement was given to similar distilleries in England, on the ground of assisting agriculture, and by the beginning of the eighteenth century all England was flooded with native as well as imported gin at absurdly low prices.

The results were most disastrous. London streets abounded with ginshops, and one could actually find placards on them reading, "Drunk for a penny; dead drunk for twopence; clean straw for nothing." The effects on the common people were so marked that all thoughtful persons were alarmed by it. In the wet, temperate climate of England people might drink heavily of beer or wine, and still in fair measure retain their health and their capacity for work; but, under the reign of gin, vice and misery and disease increased so fearfully that Parliament finally passed a law practically prohibiting its use.

This famous "Gin Law," passed in 1736, is interesting as the earliest severe blow at liquor dealing among civilized nations. It levied a tax of twenty shillings a gallon on spirits, and a license of fifty pounds for any one selling or dealing in it. And, being in advance of public opinion, it failed much as other, more stringent, prohibition laws have failed in our own day. For the cry was at once raised that it taxed the poor man's gin, and let the rich man's wine go free. Every wit, every caricaturist, had his fling at it. Ballads were hawked round, telling of the approaching death of Mother Gin. The liquor shops were hung with black, and celebrated uproariously Madame Geneva's lying in state, her funeral, her wake, and so on. The night before the law went into effect, so the contemporary journals say, there was a universal revel all over the country. Every one drank his fill, and carried home as much gin, besides, as he could pay for.

To evade the law, apothecaries sold it in vials and small packages, sometimes colored and disguised, generally under false labels, such as "Colic Water," "Make Shift," "Ladies' Delight." There were printed directions on some of these packages—e. g., "Take two or three spoonfuls three or four times a day, or as often as the fit takes you." Informers were very prominent and exceedingly offensive, inventing snares to catch lawbreakers for the sake of the heavy rewards, and spying and sneaking around in a way particularly distasteful to the English mind. In consequence, they suffered in their turn. The mere cry "Liquor spy!" was enough to raise a mob in the London streets, and the informer was lucky if he escaped with a sound thrashing and a ducking in the Thames or the nearest horse pond. Indeed, such an outcry was made about the matter that the ministry became very unpopular, and the law was not enforced after two or three years, and was largely modified in 1743, after seven years' trial.

While the lower classes in England were thus being demoralized by gin, the upper classes were suffering almost as much from the introduction of the strong, sweet, fiery, heavily brandied wines of Portugal, thanks, in part at least, to some favoring clauses in the Methuen treaty, early in the eighteenth century. It is curious to read in the contemporary journals and diaries and in the histories and descriptions of the last century—as, for instance, in Trevelyan's Life of Fox—how terribly demoralized was the state of English society during the period of England's greatest colonial and material expansion. The country was governed by a small, wealthy, land-owning aristocracy, who seemed to take the most unbridled corruption in public, and the most unrestrained dissipation in private life as a matter of course. It was from the long years of peace under the Walpoles, during the first half of the century, when the energy and industry of the middle classes were able to exert themselves, and from the protection of her insular position, that England obtained strength to master her empire, not from any superiority in her governing classes.

For, all during the last century, drunkenness was the rule, not the exception, in all classes of society. In the lower classes it was actually encouraged. Did the troops win a victory, did a prince come of age, "Go home. Jack," would say the master to his servant, "build a big bonfire, and tell the butler to make ye all drunk." It was quite a compliment to call an underling an "honest, drunken fellow."

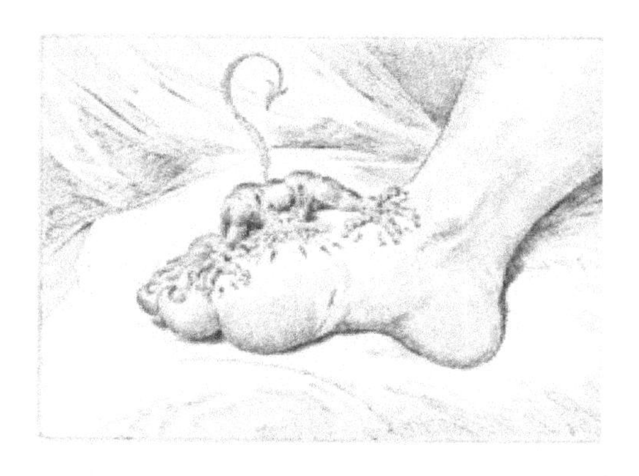

THE GOUT. (Gillray.)

And as for the gentlefolk—well, we can hardly conceive of the state of affairs. It was part of a gentleman's education to learn to carry his port. One, two, three quarts a night was a proper and reasonable supply. After dinner the ladies retired into another room—practice still observed—so that the men should have no embarrassing restraints, and it was a matter of course for them to drink one another under the table as fast as was convenient. In the army and navy, in the learned professions, among the gentry and nobility, and even in the royal family, heavy drinking was the rule and not the exception until well on in the present century.

And they suffered from it. Their lives were shortened, their usefulness impaired, their estates squandered, and then the gout! Nowadays, with the example of Palmerston and Bismarck, Gladstone and Sherman before our eyes, it is hard to think of a time when statesmen were incapacitated at thirty-five or forty. But it was so. A gentleman who reached middle age without being crippled was either unusually lucky or was a milksop. Lord Chatham and many, nay most, of his contemporaries were horribly tortured by it. At critical periods in the nation's history a severe onset of gout, or the illness leading up to it, would cause the retirement of the most prominent statesmen. Many of them died young. Few indeed of them reached a healthy and vigorous old age. For heavy drinking was not confined to the idlers and spendthrifts, the courtiers and country gentlemen; it was a custom with the ablest and most brilliant men in England.

JOHN BULL PETITIONING PITT AND DUNDAS TO LIGHTEN THE LIQUOR TAX. (Gillray.)

Pitt and Fox, the two "Great Commoners," were noted topers. The old couplet is still remembered that refers to a scene in the House of Commons when Pitt and his friend Dundas came staggering in, and Pitt says: "I can not see the Speaker, Dick; can you?" "Not see the Speaker? Hang it, I see *two*." And all through the regency and well on through the next reign until the accession of the young Queen, there prevailed what to us would seem unpardonable license.

But it must not be inferred from this that drinking was much *more* prevalent in England than in other parts of the world at the same periods. Indeed, the records of Germany and Holland show quite as startling pictures. And in our own country we have not much to boast of.

The North American Indians were, on the whole, unaccustomed to alcoholic beverages before the arrival of the white man. Tobacco they had, and used it freely. In some stray localities we read of drinks made from maize; and from the reports of Captains Amadas and Barlow to Sir Walter Raleigh about the expedition to Virginia in 1584, we find that the Indians along the coast of Chesapeake Bay and the Carolinas had learned the art of making wine from grapes. But when the Puritans landed in Massachusetts in 1620 they found, to their disgust, that beer and wine were both lacking, and we find Governor Bradford complaining bitterly of the hardship of drinking water.

Nor was water a more favored beverage among the settlers of Massachusetts Bay eight or ten years later. The first list of necessities sent back to the home company, in 1629, is headed, as our New England friends have so frequently reminded us, by an appeal for "ministers," and for a "patent under scale." We do not hear so often of their request, only a line or two further down, for "vyne planters." They ask for wheat, rye, barley, and other grains, and also for "hop rootes."

The records are still kept of the equipment of the vessel sent out in answer to this appeal. It was provisioned for one hundred passengers and thirty-five sailors for three months, each sailor counting as much as two passengers. They provided for the voyage "forty-five tuns beere, at four and six shillings per tun; two caskes Mallega and Canarie at sixteen shillings; twenty gallons aqua vitæ," and—for drinking, cooking, and all, only six tuns of water!

Higginson, the well-known first minister, went out in 1628. The next year he wrote home a glowing account of the country. Among other things, the air was so fine that his health was greatly benefited. "And whereas my stomache could only digest and did require such drinke as was both strong and stale, now I can and doe oftentimes drinke New England water verie well."

This really remarkable fact we find explained a few years after by Wood, in his New England's Prospect. He says that the country is well watered, and with different water from that of England; "not so sharpe, of a fatty substance, and of a more jetty colour. It is thought that there can be no better water in the world; yet dare I not preferre it to good Beere as some have done. Those that drinke it be as healthful, fresh, and lustie as they that drinke beere."

By 1631 they had passed a law for putting drunkards in the stocks; other laws followed concerning adulterations, sale to savages, etc. In 1634 the price of an "ale quart of beere" was set at a penny, and brew houses were soon in every village, in some places attached to every farm. The manufacture of other drinks followed rapidly, and in Judge Sewall's diary, some forty or fifty years later, we find mention of ale, beer, mead, metheglin, cider, wine, sillabub, claret, sack, canary, punch, sack posset, and black cherry brandy. The commonest of all these was "cyder," which was produced in enormous quantities and drunk very freely. Sack was passing out of date, excepting in posset, a delectable mixture of wine, ale, eggs, cream, and spices, boiled together. Metheglin and mead were brewed from one part of honey and two or two and a half parts of water and spices, fermented with yeast, and very heady liquors they were. The least excess, as they used to say, would bring back the humming of the bees in the ears. Governor Bradford early issued one of his orders against some "Merrymount scamps" on board the bark Friendship, who took two barrels of metheglin from Boston to Plymouth, and "dranke up, under the name leakage, all but six gallons."

But none of these, nor the "beveridge" and "swizzle" made from molasses and water, the perry, peachy, spruce and birch beer, and the rest, did half as much execution as rum. This was introduced from Barbadoes about 1650, and from then on became practically the national drink of the country. A great trade was set up with the West Indies, the ships exporting corn and pork and lumber for the plantations, and returning with cargoes of raw sugar and molasses, which last was almost valueless where it was made, but, diluted and fermented, furnished a ready source of alcohol.

Every little Now England town and village had its distillery—the seaport towns had scores of them—and the rum bullion, rumbooze, or, as it was universally known, killdivil, was sold freely for two shillings a gallon, and was shipped largely to the African coast in exchange for slaves. It was to this profitable trade that Newport and other New England coast towns owed their prosperity, and the interference with this trade by the English Commerce Acts was one of the main causes of the Revolution.

This rum was the basis not only of "flip," when mixed with beer, molasses, dried pumpkin, and sometimes cream and eggs, and stirred, before serving, with a red-hot poker, but also of punch. This latter, named after an East Indian word meaning five, was concocted with sugar, spices, lemon juice, and water, and was imbibed freely. As early as 1686 we find travelers telling of noble bowls of punch, which were passed from hand to hand before dinner. Double and "thribble" bowls there were also, holding two or three quarts each, and the amounts that our ancestors disposed of in those days are staggering.

For liquor was not only used at dinner and supper parties; it was taken morning, noon, and night, as a matter of course. The laborer would not work at the harvest, the builders at their trades, without a liberal allowance of rum. It did not matter, either, what class of work they were doing. When the little town of Medfield, early in the last century, "raised" the new meeting house, there were required "four barrels beer, twenty-four gallons West Indian rum, thirty gallons New England rum, thirty-five pounds loaf sugar, twenty-five pounds brown sugar, and four hundred and sixty-five lemons." A house could not be built without liquor being distributed at every stage of the operation, and this practice was not obsolete till well on in this century.

The clergy, while keeping a strict eye upon the excesses of their parishioners, did not disdain a drop themselves, and their conventions rivaled the dinners of the non-elect. In 1792 Governor Hancock gave a dinner to the Fusileers at the Merchants' Club in Boston, and for eighty diners there were served one hundred and thirty-six bowls of punch, twenty-one bottles of sherry, and lots of cider and brandy. But a similar bill is preserved for the refreshments at the ordination of a clergyman at Beverly, Mass., in 1785, and we notice:

30 Bowles Punch before they went to meeting	£3	0*s.*	0*d.*
80 people eating in morning, at 16*d*	6	0	0
10 bottles of wine before they went to meeting	1	10	0
68 dinners at 30*d*	10	4	0
44 bowles punch while at dinner	4	8	0
18 bottles wine	2	14	0
8 bowles brandy	1	2	0
Cherry Rum	1	10	0
and 6 people drank tea	0	0	9

It would be but useless repetition to discuss the drinking habits of New York and other colonies. It is enough to say that well on into the present century drunkenness was extremely common, and, when people could afford it, a most pardonable and venial offense. It is the pride of our civilization in the present century that, during the last fifty or seventy-five years, the whole tone of society has changed, and intemperance, while still unfortunately prevalent, is nothing like as common as it used to be.

Indeed, it is hardly possible for us to imagine the state of affairs in our grandfathers' times. A hundred years ago a gentleman who went out to dinner, and was not brought home in the bottom of a cab or in a wheelbarrow, was a very poor-spirited fellow indeed. So with the poorer classes. Just a century ago George Washington was engaging a gardener, and in his contract it was expressly stipulated that he should have "four dollars at Christmas, with which he may be drunk for four days and four nights; two dollars at Easter to effect the same purpose; two dollars at Whitsuntide, to be drunk for two days ; a dram in the morning, and a drink of grog at dinner at noon." Nor was the sum mentioned a niggardly one, when George Washington was distilling his own whisky, and selling it, probably, for thirty or forty cents a gallon.

And now, just think of the change. We can hardly imagine a gentleman perceptibly exhilarated with wine at a dinner table. He certainly would never get a second opportunity, if the fact were known. And as for the working classes—a clerk, an engineer, a coachman, or even a gardener whose breath smelt of whisky, or who was seen often dropping into a saloon, would run a good chance of losing his position.

For the world has at last found out what intoxication means. Alcohol in large doses is a poison, but it is a poison which injures the family and neighbors and friends of the inebriate more than the victim himself. It, to some extent at least, causes him discomfort, but think of the discomfort it causes his family! It shortens his life, to be sure, but think of the other lives that it shortens! And while some attack the problem with fierce and violent denunciations, and others by quieter and not the less effective arguments and appeals, the world certainly owes a debt of gratitude to those who are doing so much now, and who have done so much already, to relieve mankind from the burden of inebriety.

Printed in the USA
CPSIA information can be obtained
at www.ICGtesting.com
LVHW051207070724
784840LV00026BA/201